the academic warrior

Becoming a Purposeful Learner

By **ROBERT PRATT, Ph.D.**

Contributing Authors

PAULA SUNDET WOLF
KAYE TAVERNIER
KIRSTIN VAN DEN BERG

The Academic Warrior: Becoming a Purposeful Learner
 by Robert Pratt, Ph.D.

Contributing Authors
Paula Sundet Wolf, Kaye Tavernier, and Kirstin van den Berg

Student Tips
Ashley Ross and Clara Waddell

Illustrator
Kelly Dupre

Book Designer
Katherine Hellner

Published by Cook County Higher Education,
P.O. Box 57, Grand Marais, Minnesota 55604, U.S.A.
highered@boreal.org

ISBN 978-0-9833842-0-5

First Printing March, 2011

Printed in the United States of America

table of contents

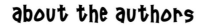

about the authors

Author

Robert E. Pratt, (Ph.D., University of Connecticut) was born and raised in Grand Marais, Minnesota. He was Director of Services for the Pretrial Diversion Project in Hartford, Connecticut and Coordinator of the Graduate program in Counselor Education at California State University, San Bernardino, California. He is Professor of Counseling Emeritus at the Minnesota State University Moorhead and has been involved in education for over 45 years.

Contributing Authors:

Paula Sundet Wolf is the Executive Director at Cook County Higher Education (CCHE), a non-profit distance education resource center in Grand Marais, MN. She is currently studying for her Ph.D. in Teaching and Learning at the University of North Dakota; her coursework is a combination of online, independent study, and cohort sessions on the campus. She has worked at CCHE for over 11 years.

Kaye Tavernier has been a special education teacher and a mathematics teacher in Cook County School District for 25 years. She is licensed to teach elementary education, secondary mathematics and special education K-12. She is a long time member of Minnesota Council of Teachers of Mathematics, serving three years as a regional representative on the board of directors. She has participated as a Minnesota Department of Education panel member multiple times in the area of Mathematics Assessment.

Kirstin van den Berg works as the Program Coordinator for Cook County Higher Education, a non-profit organization dedicated to lifelong learning. Since 2005, Ms. van den Berg has assisted hundreds of adult students in reaching their goals of career training, business development and college education. Kirstin is currently in the process of pursuing her Masters Degree in Higher Education Administration and Leadership.

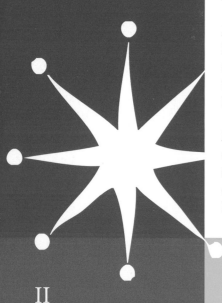

acknowledgements

This work would not have been completed without the help of many individuals. Many thanks to my wife, Bev, and my colleague at MSUM, Mary Ann (Zarrett) Hunnicutt, Ph.D. They helped get this project started after my implementation of the Academic Fitness program at MSUM. I would like to thank Paula and Kirstin at CCHE for their infinite patience in meeting the challenge of keeping me focused to complete this project. Special thanks to Kelly Dupre for the wonderful bird illustrations, and Katherine Hellner for the book design. Thanks to the many individuals too numerous to list who helped with editing and review. And also, thanks to the creative writing group who read my project and then provided feedback and suggestions.

Special thanks to my friend, John Miller, for all the support he has given me for this project.

preface

The title "*The Academic Warrior: Becoming a Purposeful Learner*" prompted a lot of discussion, enough that it is worth noting that the title is about discovering that you, as a student, have the potential to become a very *strong* student. So many of us lost our sense of academic strength through big and small experiences that made us feel stupid, insecure, and inadequate. Young girls in particular suffered under the "I can't do math" myth. The Academic Warrior is about finding your personal strength, and discovering that you are powerful, capable, and most of all intelligent. I like to think that you will imagine yourself holding a sword and shield, ready to slay your mental dragons as you tackle your assignments. Like any fit athlete, eventually the process will be less of a workout and more of a pleasure, even a passion.

I wish you success and joy in your academic ventures.

— Paula Sundet Wolf, Executive Director, Cook County Higher Education

foreword by bob pratt

I am writing this book for two reasons. First, I want to offer something to encourage and challenge students, particularly self–doubting students, to build competence and confidence by developing a strong foundation of study skills and a fighting attitude. My second reason is more personal: I face my own self–doubt when it comes to writing.

In order to accomplish reason one, I have to step up and tackle reason two. Four years before retiring from teaching and counseling at Minnesota State University Moorhead, I developed and implemented a program in study skills called Academic Fitness. My motivation to do this was stimulated by feedback from students who were struggling academically.

My purpose in developing this program was threefold:

- First, develop a no-nonsense attitude by building mental toughness and intellectual endurance.
- Second, introduce students to powerful study techniques and provide lots of practice using them.
- Third, have students begin taking more responsibility for their own learning.

Many capable students turn off to school at some point. Why? Why do many of us show up physically, but our minds are elsewhere? Perhaps there are as many reasons as there are students who tune out.

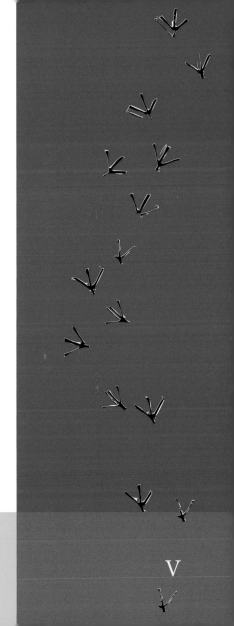

My Friend Phooey

I have a friend nicknamed "Phooey" (that's his version of swearing). Phooey, who really likes to be considered one of the boys, went out and bought a brand new Harley Davidson motorcycle — a real beauty, candy apple red, lots of chrome and loud pipes. It's a high-powered moving machine (or I should say it *could* be). Trouble is, Phooey's afraid to ride it; the bike just sits under a blanket in his garage. Oh, I should give him some credit; once in a while he takes off the blanket, sits on the Harley, starts it, revs the engine in neutral, and listens to the thunderous sound of the pipes (fantasizing about riding off to Sturgis, South Dakota), but the Harley just sits there.

Since Phooey purchased his Harley, he has developed an amazing skill at coming up with excuses for not riding his bike — "looks like rain" or "good day to go riding if it weren't so windy." We are thinking of renaming our friend "Neutral" because he just sits on his bike with all that power under him. The truth is, Phooey is going nowhere until he puts that big Harley into gear, engages the clutch and challenges himself to ride out and take on the road. It's not enough to just have it. You've got to use it.

Could this relate to you? We know you have intelligence. Now the big question is, "Do you have the courage to use it or do you want to play it safe by staying in neutral?" This is where your mental attitude comes into play, where you step up and use it, exercising your capacity to be mentally tough. You have the power. I challenge you to develop your mental stamina by facing the demands of college coursework.

The purpose of this book is to introduce you to study/learning techniques and strategies that are simple to learn and easy to apply. You will be amazed at how mentally tough you are! You will:

- Learn proven study techniques, strategies, and exercises.
- Practice and apply these techniques and strategies.
- Develop your mental grit, tenacity, and stamina.
- Use the techniques that best complement your strengths.
- Discover how the proper attitude feeds success.

introduction

You are smarter than you think. But, do you know how to put your mind to work? Having potential is one thing, knowing how to use it is another. In high school, many of us had lots of instruction in *what* to study, but little or no instruction on *how* to study. As a consequence, many students enter college lacking the skills and mental toughness essential for success in college. For example, did you learn how to:

- Read your textbooks in ways to get the most meaning from them?
- Take good notes, and know how and when to study them for maximum benefit?
- Find the power range of your memory?
- Reduce mental drift?
- Maintain focus?
- Quiz yourself to prepare for tests?
- Make good use of your dead time?

This book is written to reach out and urge you, encourage you, prod you (whatever it takes) to step up and become a more powerful learner and highly-skilled student. It is especially intended for anyone who may have some doubt about his or her ability to succeed in college. I may not know you, but I do know this, you have much more ability than you use! Yet having ability and knowing how to use it are not always the same.

"The mind is not a vessel to be filled, but a fire to be kindled."
— Plutarch

how to use this guide

I suggest you read the entire book first to get a grasp of how Parts One and Two support one another.

Part One: *Fire Up Your Mind* points out some of the excuses we may use to avoid our studies. Better yet, it suggests ways to overcome them, how to fire up your mind and tackle your studies with zest and purpose.

Part One provides a rationale for using the study techniques and strategies offered in Part Two: *Time for Tools & Study Strategies*. This section provides specific methods for tackling your studies, such as reading textbooks, taking good notes and preparing for tests.

Following your initial reading of the book, refer to any section of the guide that you would find useful toward improving your performance.

In addition to the text, there are tips and suggestions that have been offered by students throughout the guide. You will find them helpful, and you may come up with some of your own. I encourage you to share them with me at highered@boreal.org. Let's get to it!

chapter 1   my story

I was one of those students who tuned out. Starting in junior high, I was into cars, trucks, motorcycles — anything but school. I believed it was the teacher's job to make classes interesting, even entertaining. As far as school was concerned, I was setting myself up for failure.

Worse yet, I developed a cynical attitude toward learning. I would carry books home from school, only to lug them back the next morning without opening them. I might as well have been carrying bricks. The only time I cracked a book in high school was the night before a test or when someone got on my case.

Unwittingly, I had become a dedicated underachiever, highly skilled at ducking and dodging academic challenge. I had allowed myself to become an academic wimp. Having taken this route, what did I learn? I learned to believe I was stupid. This was not a good mind-set for entering college.

Living up to my self-image, I dropped out of college during my freshman year. I lacked purpose, skill, and belief in my capabilities. After returning home, I worked several jobs and married my high school sweetheart. A few years later, a fellow truck driver, Darrell, tried talking me into returning to college, but I resisted. After all, I wasn't "smart enough" for college. However, Darrell was persistent and continued to challenge me to enroll. The pivotal conversation went like this:

Darrell: *Did you write or call any colleges this weekend?*
Me: *No!*
Darrell: *Why not?*
Me: *There's no way; I have a family to support.*
Darrell: *So?*
Me: *Do you know how old I'd be by the time I graduated?*
Darrell: *How long would it take to graduate?*
Me: *I suppose four or five years; I'd have to keep working.*
Darrell: *How old will you be four or five years from now if you go to college?*
Me: *Twenty-three or twenty-four years old.*
Darrell: *Now, how damn old will you be four or five years from now if you don't go?*

When Darrell asked that last question, something flashed in my mind like "Hellooooo Bob, if you're going to be around four or five years from now, why not be here with a college degree?" This was the first time I had thought of it in that light. Suddenly, I realized that if I graduated from college, additional career opportunities would become available. I decided to give it another try.

The Big Disappointment

The night before our departure for college, my mother came to our house and asked to speak with me privately. She made a statement that I will always remember. "You will never make it through college; you have been such a disappointment all along." Over time, my actions had taught her to expect very little from me. Nevertheless, it was like being stung by a dozen bees at once.

Ironically, that statement mobilized a powerful force in me, a force I didn't even know existed. In that instant, I knew I would finish college. Nothing would stop me. The words "You'll never make it" would provide a constant source of motivation. Unleashing that force changed my attitude from a tentative **academic wimp** to an attitude of a tenacious **academic warrior**. I was determined to survive even though I didn't know *how* to study at the college level. No way was I "backing down." It was time to *push* my limits, *reclaim* my mind, and put up a darn good fight. I was ready to learn how to learn and put my mind to work.

Arriving at Mankato State College, I was still scared, but the fire burning in me was greater. No matter how tough it got, there was no turning back. Mobilized with intense purpose, I knew I would learn how to survive the demands of college. If I couldn't make it on brains, I would make it on guts and persistence.

Going to school and supporting a family was tough. I worked nights in a gas station and drove truck during the summer, while my wife worked as a waitress in a restaurant and a cashier at a supermarket.

Each time it got tough and I thought about quitting, the words, "You'll never make it through college" echoed in my mind. I *consciously* countered with my own words, "The hell I won't!" With effort and grit I began to drop my old pattern of escape and generated the tenacity to persist. I graduated four years later with a degree in, of all things, education.

20 Years Later

As a counselor and professor at Minnesota State University, Moorhead (MSUM), I talked to many students who were failing academically. Why were they failing? There seemed to be a common theme — a lack of confidence in their ability and skill to perform well at the college level. These students seemed unaware of three important facts:

- There is a whopping difference between lack of confidence in ability and the actual lack of ability.
- One can learn and become proficient in the skills necessary for academic achievement.
- When skilled, you exercise your abilities with competence and confidence.

Remembering my own experience and struggle when I first entered college, I could identify with these students, and began asking them what I could do to help. The most frequent response given was "teach us how to study." I was in a position to assist them to cultivate the necessary skills and attitudes that lead to improved learning. As a result, I designed a program that I hoped would help, and offered it to students who were on academic probation.

After introducing Academic Fitness at MSUM, I had the opportunity to work with and learn from over 300 students. Each was subject to suspension if he or she did not achieve a minimum of a C grade average for that term.

The program expanded from one group to four groups per term. When I retired four years later, over 300 students on academic probation had completed the program, 83 percent successfully — that's better than eight out of 10! I must add that these students have every reason to be very proud, since each one of them reclaimed the power of their mind and was able to continue on with his or her college education.

At the beginning of each semester, many students were hesitant to experiment with different approaches to the study process. Yet, some took the risk and began reporting improvement in test scores and grades on written assignments.

For example, a young man came to class one day and said: *"Hey, this stuff works! On my first test I got a D. I felt really stupid because I had studied hard, but I didn't know what I was doing. After practicing the study skills, I earned a high B on my next test. I think what helped the most was taking good notes and quizzing myself each day. I was no smarter, but I learned how to study smarter."*

After hearing success reported by their peers, the more reluctant students began applying these techniques to their own studies, and soon they began reporting improvement as well. Once students began earning higher grades on tests and term papers, I observed a dramatic improvement in their attitudes and actions towards studying and learning. As students continued to practice effective study strategies, they became more competent in their use and began to realize their intellectual power. Most — 83 percent over a four-year period — made dramatic improvement in their academic performances, moving from F's, D's, and C's to C's, B's, and A's. As they gained in competence, students reported a boost in confidence.

What Made the Difference?

Improvement in performance was the result of acquired study strategies and a new attitude of tenacity and persistence. Students were no more intelligent after completing the program than when they entered. However, they could apply their minds skillfully in more potent ways, as evidenced by their improved grade-point averages.

Having become better skilled in the art of learning, students displayed an attitude of openness and enthusiasm for further academic challenge.

What Does This Have To Do With You?

Even though I don't know your name, I do know something about you. I know for a fact you have far more intellectual capacity than you use. Challenge your brain. Push your limits to become a strong thinker. Don't worry about overuse. You can sprain a muscle, but you can't sprain your brain. I don't know anyone who has blown a neuron due to heavy-duty thinking.

By combining effective study strategies and a tenacious attitude towards learning, you can propel yourself into becoming a more powerful thinker. However, I must warn you, just reading this book will not make you a better student any more than reading a driver's manual will make you a better driver. To become a competent and skilled thinker, you must act upon and consciously practice study strategies that work until they become a habit. Let's begin with examining the importance of attitude.

chapter 2   IQ vs. attitude and skill

In our society, heavy emphasis is placed on the intelligence quotient (IQ), a score frequently used to predict academic performance. Too often, it is believed the major factor separating powerful students from weaker ones is superior intelligence.

This belief is misleading. IQ only denotes potential. What frequently prevents the weak student from becoming a strong student is a **(1) self-defeating attitude** toward learning and **(2) lack of skill** in knowing how to study. Both of these factors combine to put you at risk. In fact, the lack of strong study skills often leads to a self-defeating attitude towards learning. Weak study skills leave you vulnerable to inefficient and sloppy thinking.

Conversely, projecting an **assertive** attitude, coupled with skill in study strategies, invigorates your mind to tackle learning opportunities with energy and purpose. You can easily arm yourself with powerful study strategies. You can also change your attitude, often in a matter of seconds. The following chapters emphasize the development of a powerful learning attitude and cultivating skill in proven study techniques and strategies.

Attitude
Your attitude is a major contributor to your failure or success as a learner. Attitude colors your thinking and influences your actions. It serves as a driving force behind *what* and *how* you think. You make instantaneous judgments, either negative or positive, toward every academic challenge.

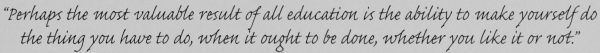

"Perhaps the most valuable result of all education is the ability to make yourself do the thing you have to do, when it ought to be done, whether you like it or not."
— Thomas Huxley

Based upon these judgments, your attitude:

- is projected onto the learning situation you are confronting (or avoiding)
- dictates how you *feel* during the study process (frustrated, anxious, bored vs. calm, alert, determined)
- influences how you *act* (avoid or engage) in the study process
- ultimately impacts your learning outcomes

No matter how intelligent you are, a negative attitude toward learning is *self-limiting*. It creates a resistance within your mind to any opportunity to succeed. In essence, you set yourself up for annoyance, frustration and disappointment. Your self-talk, founded in negativity, might go something like this: "I hate this stuff." — "It's too hard." — "I can't do it." — "Why do they make me take all these classes?" Trying to make it through college with a negative attitude is like driving a car with one foot on the accelerator and the other foot on the brake. You constantly alternate between "I can" and "I can't."

The Fallacy of "I Can't"
It's amazing that by kindergarten, children have learned to master two very difficult and complex processes: how to walk and how to talk (some come to school speaking two languages). And no wonder; most of them are cheered on by adults and experience lots of praise, even after taking a tumble.

Think about this — what if you had to wait until your current age to learn to walk and talk? What would your attitude be toward learning these two very challenging activities? Would you be eager to get started and able to practice in public? Would you be free from embarrassment and the fear of making mistakes? Would you be perfectly comfortable saying "gaga" instead of "daddy," or falling on your duff while walking into a restaurant?

The Pitfalls of Self-Doubt

How do we learn to doubt ourselves? Is this something we are told, even taught? There are many ways we learn "I can't," from the very subtle to the very blatant. These messages often come from significant people at various points in our developmental journey. It could be parents, teachers, counselors, religious leaders, siblings, or peers. It could be a result of social or economic status, or the result of low expectations. No matter where or from whom these messages have come, when we believe them without question, we are vulnerable to developing a very false and self-limiting belief system.

One of these faulty beliefs is "I can't." For example, a young college student stated that he was diagnosed with a learning disability and said, "I can't pass science classes." However, he was enrolled in a required chemistry class at the time. We discussed his situation and developed a plan consisting of some specific study strategies. He decided to be a beginning chemist and learn all he possibly could while in the course. I suggested he use the following mantra: "This is tough, but so am I." He earned a B in the class. Another student said that whenever she was told she couldn't do something, she responded with, "Oh yeah, just watch me!"

"Study without desire spoils the memory, and it retains nothing that it takes in."
— Leonardo da Vinci

Propel Yourself Forward by Erasing "I Can't"
Start telling yourself the truth by replacing "I can't" with statements that emphasize "I can" such as, *"With good thinking, I can do this"* or *"I'm going to give this my best effort."*

By generating a fighting attitude, one of vigor and strength of mind towards learning, you project yourself from a position of power, approaching your studies with total purpose. Self-talk would likely go something like this: "I'm going to give this my best shot. I'm going to focus my attention and test my limits. I will learn this material so well I'll be able to teach it to someone else." With an alert, energetic attitude, you engage your mind with clarity and purpose.

Attitude is something over which you have tremendous control. When it comes to studying, you can make your attitude your enemy or your ally. It's your **choice**! You can take the so-called easy route and allow yourself to perform poorly by applying a negative attitude to your studies. Or, you can consciously choose to be an academic warrior by taking command of your mind and tenaciously tackling any academic challenge that comes your way. A determined attitude, combined with knowing how to study with skill, make a powerful contribution to student success.

Developing the tenacity to confront tough academic challenges and persisting until they are conquered requires an attitude of intellectual courage. Think about why you wanted a college education in the first place. Take on the challenge.

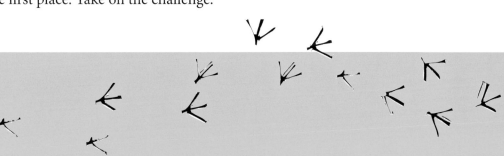

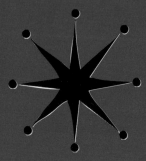

Food for Thought

Snacks distract you from studying. Studying is work and needs your concentration. Save healthy snacks for your break.

Drink plenty of water or mint tea to keep your mind sharp.

Show Your Mental Grit

Don't kid yourself, it takes guts to sit down and study a difficult subject. You are moving from the comfort of the known into the discomfort of the unknown.

Put yourself in this scenario: you are enrolled in a course (for example, economics), a subject that requires rigorous mental effort. You know it is in your best interest to begin reading your econ text right now. You face a decision. Which are you most likely to do? Check your e-mail, or sit down to open your book and start reading? Show your mental tenacity by remaining highly focused and on task for 20 minutes.

Exercise 1: Challenge Your Mental Toughness

*This challenge begins **after** you finish a reading assignment. Muster up the mental toughness to quiz yourself for 10 minutes over what you have just read. Like top-notch athletes pushing their physical limits, you can push, stretch, and extend your intellectual limits by quickly quizzing yourself over the material you just covered. This is the time to discover what you know, as well as what you don't know. At this point, you can go back and pick up the information that you previously missed.*

Think about it! *Any* challenge requires you to sacrifice some immediate comfort and contains an element of risk. There is no guarantee everything (or anything) will turn out well. If you were guaranteed success, it wouldn't be a challenge. It requires a lot of maturity to initiate and sustain mental effort.

Three of your best resources are your *mind, courage*, and *persistence*. Use them and experience the best that is in you. As one Academic Fitness student stated "Hey, college ain't for mental wimps!"

chapter 3   becoming an academic warrior

Commit yourself to becoming an academic warrior. Everyone has choices. You can consciously choose to discover and exercise the full power of your mind. By activating an eager attitude combined with potent study strategies, a striking change takes place: you become an academic warrior.

What is an Academic Warrior?
Academic warriors stand up for themselves. They choose to challenge their minds. Academic warriors learn what works and do it.

As an academic warrior, you consciously activate your mind, choosing to be alert, purposeful, and focused. It takes effort to be a good thinker, to mentally wrestle with an academic challenge until you pin it down.

By choosing to be an academic warrior, you dare to take intellectual risks by confronting what you don't know with the full power of your mind. You carefully *condition* yourself through purposeful practice to become a critical thinker. Through practice, you will develop mental stamina, intellectual skill, and strong habits of the mind.

Being an academic warrior requires you to remain highly focused. When distracted, you immediately redirect your attention back on target. You tenaciously persist in narrowing the gap between what you know and what you don't know. You learn to accept, even welcome, mild discomfort that can accompany new learning. Instead of reacting emotionally to new ideas you practice *thinking* through new material.

I asked two students who had completed the Academic Fitness program, "What do you believe separates you from other students?" The following responses were given:

"I've learned to be comfortable being uncomfortable. I melt away my confusion with strong effort and thought."

"I'm learning that the way to recognize my abilities is to challenge them. Challenge keeps my mental edges sharp."

With conscious practice, active thinking becomes a rewarding habit. As an academic warrior, you experience the personal satisfaction of your own achievement. The academic warrior is:

- a courageous, gutsy thinker
- a reasoner who thinks through to solutions
- undaunted by internal or external influences
- an insatiable learner
- highly focused in the moment
- curious, raises and answers questions
- mentally tenacious — staying alert and on task
- an effective manager of time, energy, and concentration

Will You Be an Academic Warrior? The Choice Is Yours!

During discussions with students about the relationship between intelligence and student performance, students usually indicated that good thinking demands superior intelligence.

However, when asked, "Have you ever known a student who had the reputation of being highly intelligent, but was not a strong student?" Most often students answered, "yes." Then, when asked if they ever knew a student who appeared to be rather average in intelligence, but whose performance was usually high, they answered "yes" again.

One student, whose highest grade was a D, said, "*I guess I'm not college material.*" I challenged his thinking by asking for the evidence. Initially he became defensive, stating, "*College is boring as hell and run by a bunch of arrogant nerds.*" For purposes of discussion, I inquired:

> "*Instead of college boring you, could it be that you are boring yourself? What would your life be like if you chose to interest yourself in your studies, even if you think your professors are arrogant nerds?*"

He said he hadn't thought about it from that perspective. As our discussion continued, he dropped his defensiveness and became very insightful, "*When you stop to think about it, my way of studying is a prescription for poor performance no matter how smart I may be.*"

He agreed to change his attitude and get serious about learning and practicing effective study strategies. Wanting to find his limits, he made a commitment to push his mind to the max. He earned two C's and a B for his final grades. The next semester he carried four classes and earned three B's and an A.

What was different? He *chose* to become a powerful thinker with intense purpose. He developed a set of study strategies, practiced using them, and discovered that a person with self-described average intelligence *could* do well in college. He realized that college requires time, effort, and skill. He had become an academic warrior.

I have witnessed hundreds of so-called "below average" students turn their grades from D's and F's to C's, B's and A's. I know it's possible.

Potential Barriers to Learning
There are a lot of barriers or roadblocks we encounter in life. These barriers also appear in study situations. You can *allow* the following obstacles to keep you out of the game. Watch out! These can trip you up — grab you and toss you for a loop — but only if you let them. They include:

- self-doubt
- exaggerated fear of failure
- escapism
- misguided opinions and prejudices
- distractions

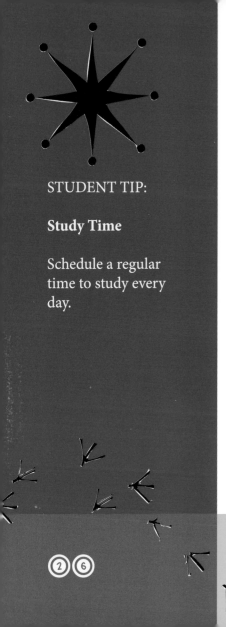

Self-Doubt

Self-doubt leads to unwarranted distrust in your ability to wrestle with college material. Too often, when things are difficult, you can allow self-doubt to creep in. This is largely created by your own self-talk. Often this self-talk is unrealistic and overly exaggerated. Yet when it goes unchallenged, it can interfere with opportunities to learn. The following are typical examples of self-defeating talk and self-enhancing talk (warrior talk).

Self-defeating talk: "This is too tough. No way could I figure it out. I'm just not college material, so why even try." Self-talk like this promotes failure. Warrior responses stand opposed to that of the doubter. They challenge self-defeating thoughts.

Warrior talk: "This is tough, but I'm tough, too. I am going to be calm and think my way through." Warriors often use self-doubt as a *trigger to exercise rational thought* in order to think and reason their way through academic challenges.

Exercise 2: Summarize for Comprehension

When studying biology, for example, act as if you are a beginning biologist, eager to learn as much as you can. Remember, when beginning anything new, allow yourself to struggle at first. Select a class where you doubt yourself, and think and act as if you are in that career and want to learn all you can. Study this subject for 15 minutes and summarize what you just learned.

Exaggerated Fear of Failure

A common barrier to academic study is anxiety, the fear of taking on a new body of knowledge and failing. When confronted with this challenge, it is easy to overreact emotionally and avoid mental effort. Many students are unwilling to tolerate even mild discomfort and are masters at avoiding academic challenge. To reduce anxiety, ask yourself, "How can biology hurt me?" Answer: "It can't, I am only scaring myself."

Calm down; focus on the task one second at a time. *Reason* your way through your assignments. Academic warriors use their discomfort to spur them on toward achieving clarity and meaning. They gain satisfaction from the actual thinking/learning process that leads to the completion of a goal. Consequently, warriors are continuously testing and honing their academic potential. Sometimes comfort is overrated!

Exercise 3: Reading and Rehearsing for Understanding

Now is the time to exercise your courage. Choose a subject that you tend to put off, open your book, read for five minutes, and then ask yourself, "What did I learn?" Remember, this is your first attempt, so give yourself some slack. Now repeat this process and read for 10 minutes. Then stop and ask, "What did I learn?" Reflect upon what you just read and write out your answer. Don't worry about spelling or grammar; just get your ideas down.

Reading and rehearsing small chunks of information strengthens learning and your ability to retain information while reducing anxiety. Rehearsal by writing strengthens retention and understanding even more.

Escapism

Escapism is behavior you engage in while you are actually in the process of studying (or think you are). Escape often occurs without your being aware that it is even happening. For example, while in class it is easy to escape by daydreaming, looking up at the clock on the wall, or paying attention to that annoying fly buzzing around the room. While reading a challenging textbook, it's also easy to drift away and start thinking about last night's party. When in the escape mode, you are present physically and absent mentally.

Warriors become aware of this natural tendency toward escapism and understand the need to remain mentally alert and focused. They consciously practice focusing total attention on their work. As soon as their attention begins to drift, they catch themselves and bring their minds back on topic.

Exercise 4: Focusing Your Concentration

Time yourself for 10 minutes of study; each time your mind drifts or is distracted, place a check mark on a sheet of paper. At the end of 10 minutes, count the check marks and take a two-minute break. Repeat the process and see if you can improve by REDUCING the number of check marks.

Misguided Opinions and Prejudices

Biased, prejudicial thinking and unsubstantiated opinions can easily get in your way. You can prejudge a subject, textbook, professor, or even your own ability with little or no evidence to support your position. For example you might say, "I am going to hate biology because I got poor grades in high school," or "I know my math professor is a jerk because he flunked my roommate." Avoid putting ignorance or biased thinking in your path to learning. Work at making objective, reasoned assessments. Rather than entering something new with a narrow perspective, give yourself a fresh start by keeping an open mind.

Self-statements are an excellent way to make objective, open-minded assessments. Some examples are:

"I am going to learn this so well I could teach it."

"Despite my present opinion, I'm going to learn the facts."

"Even though I hate biology, I am going to buckle down and persist at giving it my best effort."

Exercise 5: Creating Self-Statements

Create three of your own self-statements. Write them down and practice applying them to a personal bias or situation.

STUDENT TIP:

Give yourself a fresh start - keep an open mind.

Become Inaccessible
Find a place to study where friends can't find you.

If studying late at night, don't study near a TV. You can easily be distracted or fall asleep.

Turn off your cell phone. Read your text, but don't text!

Common Distractions

Now let's take a look at some ever-present distractions that will tantalize, tempt or entice; anything that hooks your attention and lures you off course. These are common, everyday teasers to which you are always vulnerable. These distractions can be external or intrinsic, blatant or subtle, and seem to appear out of nowhere. Distractions include:

- phone calls, TV, radios, stereos
- the sound of the refrigerator motor triggering impulses to get something to eat or drink
- the sight of a soft couch or bed creating the urge for a nap
- someone walking by
- the smell of coffee brewing
- the party downstairs

This list could go on in a never-ending chain. Staying focused and on task requires you to remain alert. Practice making a conscious choice between pursuing distractions or focusing on your tasks. Distractions have an amazing way of popping into awareness just before you sit down to study. Snuff them out before they lead you off target!

Bogus Distractions
These distractions burst into your awareness just as you are about to sit down to study.

For example:

- The plants need watering.
- I didn't get the car washed.
- My room is filthy.
- I haven't done my laundry for two weeks.
- I haven't checked my e-mail today.

Bogus distractions are tasks that have been successfully avoided in the past, but in the face of studying seem important. These sudden bursts of awareness make a strong appeal to your vulnerability. You need to be wary and alert to avoid their lure. When it's time to sit down and study, become aware of the thoughts and images that occupy your mind and compete with studying. What activity wins out?

Exercise 6: Thinking About Your Thinking
Ask yourself, "What am I thinking and doing right now? Is my mind focused on my studying or drifting away? What part is winning, the distraction or my focus?" List specific times when you are most vulnerable to distractions.

Responding to Barriers and Distractions

Academic warriors have the same distractions as everyone else. It's no easier for warriors to get out of bed and off to their first class in the morning, but they do, every morning. Warrior's textbooks are no less challenging to read, but get read, on schedule. Term papers are written, proofread, polished, and submitted when due. While others are sidetracked by problems, warriors are busy solving them.

Like athletes who practice and perfect the skills of their sports, academic warriors choose "mind workouts," rehearsing and refining the skills of disciplined study. Through the process of daily academic workouts, warriors become sharper, clearer thinkers. Workouts soon become routine, with habits of skillful thinking and efficient study emerging along with increased stamina and endurance. Lifting weights builds physical strength and stamina; likewise, mental workouts build mind power, better concentration and intellectual stamina. Warriors thrive on *tackling* new information, *generating* questions about it, and *answering* these questions.

As an academic warrior, you become as interested in the process (the how-to) of studying as you are in the end result. Take time to learn and practice using the tools, techniques and strategies introduced in Part Two of this book that make your study time more productive and rewarding.

Energy and effort are devoted to developing efficient and effective study skills. You will need to ask yourself questions and place demands on yourself to think out the answers. For example ask, "How can I make the most sense of this," or "What is the best way to move this knowledge from the book into my mind, and keep it there for future use?"

The goal is to become a skillful, well-disciplined thinker who values the process of learning, reasoning, and problem solving. Learn to enjoy the process, rather than just focusing on the resulting grade. By persistently practicing effective approaches to study, you will develop intellectual competence and stamina. In essence, as a warrior you tenaciously cultivate, hone, and strengthen your thinking/study behavior required for optimal learning and academic competence.

By now it's clear that being an Academic Warrior is due to factors largely under your control. These factors are attitude and skill:

- **Attitude** is a major contributor to your success or failure as a learner.
- **Skill** permits you to apply your thinking effectively to the study process.

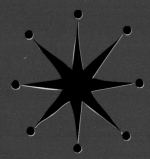

STUDENT TIP:

Stretch!

During breaks, take time to stretch your arms and legs. Do an exercise routine. And exercise your eyes by focusing on distant objects and slowly moving your eyes across the horizon.

Fact: You are born with far more intellectual ability than you use. No matter what your intellectual capacity, you seldom exercise your mind to its fullest potential. You cannot choose how intelligent you are any more than you can choose your height or the size of your feet. However, like the athlete training for his/her sport, you can commit to a rigorous **academic workout** routine, exercising your mind, building intellectual stamina and skill to peak your academic performance.

The issue is not one of ability, but using your ability to propel yourself toward more powerful learning. Choose a tough mental attitude.

Test your stamina. Become so skilled in effective study strategies that you make the very most of the ability you do possess. You are highly capable of becoming an Academic Warrior. You deserve the very best you are capable of giving yourself. Wherever you are today, you can improve. It's up to you, so choose where you want to be.

chapter 4   let's get honest

Who's in charge of your life? Do you run the show or does the show run you? As you have just read, distractions like sudden urges to get a cup of coffee, take a nap, get a snack or the sound of the TV in the next room can pull you away from your task. These distractions appear to take charge of your thoughts and actions. If you find yourself automatically acting on these impulses, you are allowing the show to run you.

Take Charge
By taking charge of your attention, you run the show and you know it! Being in charge, while studying, puts you in command of what you think and do. You have a clear purpose and devote your entire attention to your studies. Focus on your task. Make that your conscious choice.

Here are some steps to put yourself in charge:

- Select a subject to study.
- Know your purpose for studying.
- Estimate the amount of material to cover.
- Specify a time frame in which to cover the material.
- Build in 25 to 50 percent of your time to review and self-quiz.

"A goal without a plan is just a wish."
— Antoine de Saint-Exupery

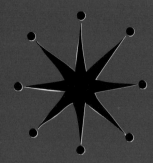

STUDENT TIP:

Study something
every day.

Avoid waiting until the
day before a test to ask
your teacher questions
about the material.

Exercise 7: Taking Charge of Your Attention
Select a difficult subject to study and notice any distractions that suddenly appear in your mind. Which distractions do you give the most power? What are you likely to do?

Now try the next exercise!

Exercise 8: Applying Your Concentration Skills
Study your textbook for one hour. Break the reading into three, 12-minute sets with a three-minute period between each set to re-state the material in your own words. After the third reading session, spend five minutes reviewing and listing the key points in your notebook. After listing the key points, write for 10 minutes describing what you learned. Write without stopping (forget grammar and punctuation), to keep your mind working and your thoughts flowing.

Advantages of Staying Focused and On Task
- You are clear on what you set out to accomplish; how you are going to get there and where your mind is, on or off task, at any point in time.
- You reduce mind wandering or falling victim to distractions and impulses.
- A clear purpose makes it easier to get started and keep moving, aware that you only have to remain focused just this second, right now.

Before you know it, you will have connected several well-focused seconds into a flow that becomes more and more automatic. When you become distracted, just take a moment and redirect your attention back on task.

chapter 5   don't blame "it"

Changing Your Personal Power From "I Can't" to "I Will!"

It's very easy to lose our power to negative emotions such as frustration, anxiety or boredom. In fact, we do this much of the time without knowing it, let alone knowing how we do it. The following steps point out how we give up our power, and better yet, show how to reclaim it.

Many students have exaggerated fear of certain academic subjects. One subject often cited is math. They make the claim that math "stresses" them. This stress is often reported as anxiety. Let's take a look at this, step by step:

Level 1: Blame. "It (math) makes me stressed."
Interpreted this way, the cause of your stress is math.

Level 2: Ownership. "I get stressed over math."
Dropping the "t" from "it" and you're left with "I." Note that "I" am the source of my stress, rather than "it" or math. Thus, you begin to own your reaction to math.

Both levels 1 and 2 are automatic reactions, which leaves the door closed to options. Therefore, you give up your power without a fight or a question. In effect, you become a helpless victim, stuck with your discomfort.

"It's not the things in life that upset us, it's the view we take of them."
— Epictetus (55 AD - 135 AD)

Level 3: Responsibility. "I *allow* myself to get stressed over math."
At level 3, you begin taking responsibility for your response. The key phrase is "I allow myself." You begin to reclaim your power.

Level 4: Activate. "I *stress myself* over math".
At level 4, you reclaim more of your power as you become increasingly aware that the cause of your stress (anxiety, frustration, etc.) resides within you. In other words, you automatically trigger your own stress by thinking false statements like, "I can't handle math" or worse yet, "Math makes me feel stupid." If we believe these messages, we create barriers within ourselves, often resulting in the "I can't" attitude towards learning. With this awareness, you are able to reduce your stress by generating new and different responses to math.

Level 5: Choice. "Rather than being stressed, I choose to be calm, objective, and thoughtful."
At level 5, you *consciously* create well-reasoned thoughts and *deliberately* say them to yourself. For example, "I can handle this, just slow down, focus one second at a time, and think my way through this." By doing this you can consciously create preferred responses and experiment with them. For this to become automatic, you have to practice.

At Level 5, you may want the help of a counselor or learning specialist who is willing to challenge your self-limiting thought processes and reactions.

Student Stories

A student who reported math anxiety shared the following:

"Rather than hurrying and worrying, I chose thinking and reasoning to beat my fear of math. I told myself, math is tough, but I am going to step up and be tougher! I took charge by telling myself to calm down and think this through. "It" worked, oops, sorry about that, 'I' worked. I passed algebra, earning a B-. More importantly, I learned that I can perform well under pressure when I practice thinking and reasoning."

Another student reported he *uses* his stress to his advantage (in this case, frustration):

"I separate myself from anxiety and frustration by using my frustration. I choose to get down in the mud and wrestle with a tough problem until I pin it. At times I've come close to being pinned myself, but I take a short break for a minute or two and go back at it again until I win. I ain't been beat yet!"

As you can see by the examples above, there are several ways you can deal with stress, and possibly use your stress to your advantage. Once you become skilled at this, you don't have to go through all the steps, you can just choose self-determination and critical thinking. And of course, this isn't just for math, but applies to all of your subjects.

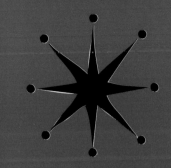

STUDENT TIP:

Keep On Top of Your Work

Procrastination creates a panic mindset that makes it extremely difficult to study with a clear head.

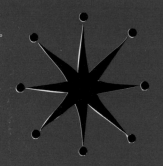

Studying with friends can provide a good way to review and quiz each other if you stay focused on the material.

Make sure you are well organized and have the same goals.

chapter 6 critical thinking

Critical Thinking is rational well reasoned thinking. As a critical thinker you cultivate and practice being open minded, curious, objective, self-directed and purposeful in your thinking. Critical thinking extends well beyond personal bias, or opinion, to positions based upon factual evidence.

Critical thinkers are skeptical, not allowing themselves to be gullible or easily persuaded by individuals or groups claiming to be an authority. Rather than swallow something "hook line and sinker" or simply going along with the crowd, critical thinkers seek information from a variety of sources representing different perspectives on a topic. Once informed, you weigh, analyze, reflect upon the facts, and develop a position based upon sound evidence.

When practicing critical thinking, you approach challenging ideas, issues and problems with enthusiasm and purpose, extending beyond and penetrating below a mere surface understanding. You become a deeper thinker, going beyond just memorizing and regurgitating information to comprehending the meaning, learning how to apply, analyze, synthesize and evaluate what you have learned. You exercise, if you will, a "head first" approach, actively thinking, asking questions, gathering information, formulating answers, and separating facts from opinion.

Critical thinkers are able to detach emotionally, remaining calm and objective, while collecting analyzing and evaluating information. As a critical thinker you practice mental courage, stepping out of your comfort zone to THINK your way through complex material, exercising reason over emotion, while remaining focused and on point.

Critical thinking is very consistent with the levels of thinking described in Bloom's Taxonomy (Benjamin Bloom, 1956), and is designed to facilitate higher-order learning. Bloom's Taxonomy, describes six levels of thinking, ranging from **knowledge** (rote memory — the lowest level on the taxonomy), to **evaluation** (making judgments, based on stringent criteria — the highest level on the taxonomy). If applied and practiced as intended, you as a learner are likely to achieve a much deeper understanding and find the learning process more interesting and satisfying.

To practice critical and purposeful thinking requires considerable mental effort. Yet I cannot recommend anything which results in more personal and long lasting satisfaction. I encourage you to step up and meet the challenge.

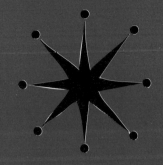

STUDENT TIP:

Sitting near the front of the class is the best spot to be able to listen actively.

bloom's taxonomy: six levels of thinking

Cognitive Skills	Definition	Examples	Key Words
Knowledge	Recall facts, data, and information	Recite poetry, chart data or facts, know rules	Define, repeat, label, memorize, name
Comprehension	Summarize, interpret, understand meaning	Explain something in your own words	Review, describe, discuss, explain
Application	Apply information to a new situation with similar circumstances	Solve problems, construct a model, draw a map, write a book	Apply, demonstrate, solve, experiment, modify
Analysis	Separate whole into parts to understand relationships	Conduct an investigation with supportive evidence, explain patterns of meaning	Analyze, calculate, compare, contrast, classify
Synthesis	Forming new concepts from a combination of information	Develop new ideas, discuss "what if" situations, revise a work manual	Design, plan, create, predict, adapt, substitute
Evaluation	Make judgments based on criteria	Select the most efficient solution, use survey results to make changes	Survey, assess, measure, justify, summarize, select, estimate, choose

"To repeat what others have said, requires education; to challenge it, requires brains."
— Mary Pettibone Poole

Here is an example of how Bloom's Taxonomy could be applied to a political science course of study:

Knowledge – What are the names of the two major political parties in the U.S.?

Comprehension – What is a political party (describe/explain)?

Application – As a member of a political party, you are asked to schedule a political caucus. Your task is to name the date, time, location, and topics to be discussed. How would you organize and publicize the event?

Analysis – Compare and contrast the two parties. How are they alike? How do they differ?

Synthesis – Imagine yourself creating a structure that would facilitate a process of reopening discussion and debate on issues that have reached a deadlock between the two parties. How would your structure lead to reopening debate between the two parties?

Evaluation – How would you evaluate the effectiveness of your plan? What criteria would you use to measure its effectiveness?

Example: Using Bloom's Taxonomy in your Sociology class

The concept you are trying to learn is "cultural diffusion". In short, cultural diffusion is the process in which a product, idea, invention, or other idea is borrowed from a foreign source and occurs when two people from different cultures make contact. Here is how you might apply Bloom's Taxonomy.

Knowledge:

What is cultural diffusion? Define cultural diffusion . . .

Describe cultural diffusion . . .

Make a list of key ideas and facts about cultural diffusion . . .

Comprehension:

Describe and write in your own words what cultural diffusion is . . .

Explain to a fellow classmate what cultural diffusion is . . .

Application:

Give examples of products and ideas that have been borrowed from a foreign source . . .

List three countries that have benefited from cultural diffusion . . .

Analysis:

Compare cultural diffusion between industrialized and non-industrialized countries . . .

Identify and explain some problems that might result from cultural diffusion . . .

List the pros and cons of cultural diffusion . . .

"An education isn't how much you have committed to memory, or even how much you know. It's being able to differentiate between what you do know and what you don't." — Anatole France

Synthesis:

   Make a list of products and ideas that might be suitable for cultural diffusion . . .
   Rate which of your products might be the most desirable . . .
   Can you imagine what an inventor might feel if he or she saw their product in another country illegally?

Evaluation:

   Do you think cultural diffusion is a good thing? Explain your reasoning . . .
   Is all cultural diffusion positive?
   Should cultural diffusion be prevented in some instances? Can cultural diffusion be prevented?

hint:

Think about things that you consider "normal" to your culture and start questioning their origins. For instance: pizza, spaghetti, ice cream, tomatoes, potatoes, popcorn, cheese, and many other food items. What about building styles, materials, techniques? How about medicines and technology? And of course plants (many of which are food plants), such as wheat, rice, corn, and squash, and decorative plants such as flowers and trees. When you consider all of these items in light of cultural diffusion, you start understanding how history, economics, and world events tie together, and the learning experience becomes personal and pertinent.

part two: time for tools and study strategies

chapter 7   memory and mind workouts

We all know that memory is vital to learning, retaining, and recalling information. Yet, have you ever been taught *how* to study in ways that utilize the strength of your memory? Have you been taught how to use your memory in ways that make the learning process more efficient and meaningful? I'll bet not. First, we need to consider why we forget information.

Many students believe they have a poor memory. This is a myth. *We are designed to forget.* Forgetting serves a very useful purpose. It keeps us from overloading our memory with useless information, leaving more memory space for useful information. Typical reasons why we forget:

- We don't pay close attention from the start.
- We delay reviewing and mind workouts (covered later in this chapter) until just before test time, then cram and overload our working memory.
- We study without a strategy.

We begin forgetting information within seconds of hearing or reading it. In fact, immediately after learning new material, if you quickly rehearse it, you will significantly boost your retention. The first 24 hours after taking in new material are critical! When you receive new information without processing it in some meaningful way, you are likely to forget approximately 40 to 50 percent or more within 24 hours. Passing a course with a 50 to 60 percent retention rate is about as realistic as expecting a good night's rest on a leaky air mattress.

Harness Your Memory

Learn how to use this powerful resource for optimal learning. Establish a basic understanding of memory, its strengths and limitations. Armed with this basic understanding, you can practice thinking and study strategies to:

- improve comprehension
- enhance meaning and relevancy
- increase retention
- strengthen your ability to retrieve and report what you have learned
- make connections and discover relationships to previous learning
- transfer new learning to future applications
- make studying and learning more enjoyable

Think About This Scenario

You spend an hour reading a chapter in your psychology textbook. After reading for about five to ten minutes your mind begins to wander. Yet you push on until you complete the chapter. Breathing a sigh of relief, you close the book, feeling pretty good about having finished the chapter, even understanding the content, for the most part. So you decide to reward yourself with a snack and TV time before hitting the sack.

STUDENT TIP:

Keep your course syllabus handy for reference throughout the course term.

It will help you keep track of assignment deadlines and test dates.

The next morning a friend comes by and asks what you did last night. You, feeling rather smug about your accomplishment, tell your friend that you read a chapter in your psych book. Being the curious type, she says, "Tell me what you learned."

You pause and recall something about classical and operant conditioning. Your friend is intrigued and says, "Wow, sounds interesting, tell me more! How is one different from the other?"

Trying to answer, you sputter like a car on empty. Each time you try to pull something profound from your memory bank, you draw a blank. The tank you thought you had filled last night has gone dry. How could that be? After all, you just read it. How could you have forgotten it so soon? It happens automatically.

What to Do
Start taking steps that promote understanding and retention. Studying *hard* is not enough. Learn how to study *smarter* and *more skillfully* to become a more powerful learner. You can do it! In the imagined scenario above, you read and perhaps understood the material. However, when you finished reading and closed the book, you left out two very critical steps: **review** and **mind workouts**. Both play an important role in the study/learning process. What is the difference between a review and a mind workout? How do you use each to your advantage?

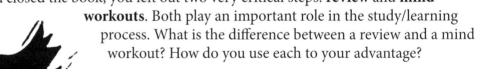

Review

Review is just what it says. You review by rereading or scanning *outside* sources like your textbook or lecture notes. The act of reviewing may aid in committing information to memory, even leave you feeling that you know the material cold. However, don't delude yourself. You have no hard evidence of what you actually know. Just because you read, understood, and reviewed something doesn't guarantee you will retain it or be capable of accurate recall. To provide evidence on what you have learned, you have to process it in some manner beyond review. That's why we add the missing link — mind workouts. Reading and remembering what you read without a mind workout is about as effective as trying to hold water in a grocery cart.

Mind Workouts

Mind workouts, often the missing link in the study process, differs from review, because the information comes from *within* your mind. You rely totally on the strength of your mind to recall, in your own words, the information just studied. Mind workouts provide evidence of what you actually do and don't know.

Mind workouts consist of any steps you take that require you to report an answer to a question, either verbally or in writing. In essence, you test yourself by raising questions and generating answers. By doing this following your daily reading and review of class lecture notes, you develop deeper understanding and meaning of the new material. You begin to move information into long-term memory, where it is more permanently stored for better retention and easier recall. Without a mind workout immediately following your study session, you are vulnerable to rapid forgetting.

STUDENT TIP:

Studying with a partner can provide a good way to review material.

However, do not rely on it as your only study method.

Mind workouts require clarity of purpose. Just before your next study session, specify what you want to accomplish, set a realistic time frame to achieve it, then test yourself in order to know what you have achieved.

Exercise 9: Test Your Recall

Without rereading the "Typical reasons why we forget," recall at least two of the three reasons. How did you do? Forgetting requires no effort, but recalling information requires focus, a mind workout and review.

Scheduling Mind Workouts
Build in time *during* each study session to mentally work out by reciting and/or writing down in your own words what you have learned. Timing of mind workouts is critical for powerful use of memory.

Three optimal times are:

- immediately after taking in a small block of information
- at the conclusion of a study session
- spaced practice over a period of time – this increases retention as learning and recall strengthens with each workout

Mix it Up

The following examples are different ways to work out with new information. These techniques and strategies provide additional ways to show evidence of what you know and what you don't know:

- self-quiz from notes
- use 3 x 5 note cards
- create mind maps (see pages 68-69)
- write summaries
- study with groups or partners
- teach someone else

Be Absolutely Clear!

Remember that review consists of returning to external sources of information, such as textbooks or lecture notes, to familiarize yourself with information you have previously studied. However, review does not provide solid evidence of what you know. On the other hand, a mind workout demonstrates what you recall without external sources, what you know, and what you still need to study.

big difference!

The Power of Prime Time

There are two times during a study period when you are likely to learn and retain the most content. The first occurs at the beginning of the session. The second time occurs at the end of the session. Material *between* the early part of a learning session and the latter part is often more difficult to remember, if not lost altogether. Imagine this: you are going to read your sociology text for one hour. You begin reading and find it interesting, but soon your mind begins to drift. Yet you continue on until just before the hour is up, and your focus becomes clearer as you reach the end of the session. Although you may recall what you read at the beginning and end of your reading, you are likely to have lost information from the middle. *This is commonly referred to as the primacy-recency effect* (Ebbinghaus, 2010, original work published 1885).

Take full advantage of your study time by working with small blocks of information at a time (for example, until your mind starts drifting) to promote rapid learning, stronger retention, and recall. For example, try reading your text for 12 minutes, and then reflect on the information for 3 minutes. During that reflection, answer the following questions: "What were the key points?" "What do they mean?" Check your answer(s) for correctness, then move on to the next section. Repeat the process for each section you read. By breaking an hour of study into smaller chunks of information and quickly quizzing yourself, you keep your mind focused.

At the conclusion of a chapter or study session, do a quick review. Following the review, take 10 to 15 minutes to write a brief summary of what you learned during the study session. Start out with something like "This is what I learned…" and write non-stop for approximately 10 to 15 minutes. Writing it out is like putting your money in the bank in order to withdraw it later, versus throwing it away.

STUDENT TIP:

Study in small blocks of time, doing reading, rehearsing, and review for optimal learning.

Adopt New Study Habits

Old study habit frequently used by students:

Recall of information is weak or lost using this old study habit.

Read	12 minutes
Reflect	3 minutes
Read	12 minutes
Reflect	3 minutes
Read	12 minutes
Reflect	3 minutes
Summarize	15 minutes

take a break!

An example of a *New* study habit to improve memory retention: With the new study habit, information from each 15-minute block of study time is better retained. You may need shorter or longer blocks of time depending on the material you are reading and your attention span.

Other Workout Options:

- Draw a mind map (see pages 68-69).
- Teach someone what you just learned.

Get in the habit of mind workouts (rehearsing) one way or another before concluding each study session. Mix up your workout strategies to avoid boredom.

These strategies can also be applied to lecture notes. Do a workout by quizzing yourself over your lecture notes as soon after class as possible and again at spaced intervals. Use this system every two to three days for new information and approximately once a week as information becomes more firmly stored in long-term memory. Distributed workouts — over time, maintain retention and increase depth of understanding while recall strengthens with each workout.

Weekly Self-Quizzes – Pre-Exams

Don't wait for your instructor(s) to test you! Create your own questions first and quiz yourself in preparation for the instructor's test. At the end of each week, construct a self-quiz. Pull questions from your lecture notes and any textbook notes generated during the past week. Typical self-quizzes range from 10 to 15 questions per week, for each class. Save your weekly self-quizzes and combine them to provide preparation for course exams. After two or three weeks, you could easily have 30 to 50 questions you have developed and already used to

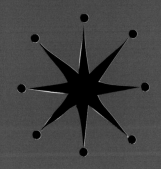

STUDENT TIP:

Tutoring other people in a subject you are currently studying is a great way for you to gain in-depth knowledge and understanding of the material.

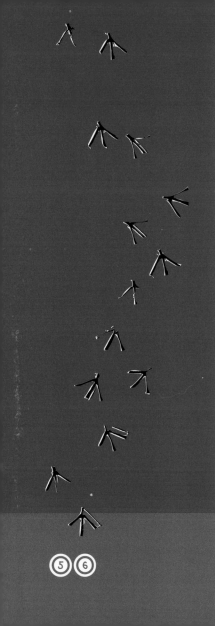

quiz yourself. By exam time you will probably have answered more practice questions than your instructors will ask on official examinations.

Avoid Cramming

Last-minute cramming can overload working memory, resulting in rapid memory fade, impairing your recall. You wouldn't think of running a marathon by cramming your training in two days before the race, yet many students procrastinate until the last minute and overload their working memory by cramming just before a test. To maximize your readiness for a test, it is smart to schedule several short workout sessions (mini tests) throughout the term, prior to test time. Refer to the Study/Rehearse/ Workout Cycle and Weekly Self-Quiz described in Chapters 10 and 11.

Focused attention

Focused attention means you deliberately keep your mind concentrated on a specific task. Why is focus important? Think about it. What happens when playing a sport or driving a car, if you lose focus, allowing your mind to drift for just a second?

Story: When I was a kid I went to a basketball game. The team I was cheering for was ahead by two points. Their star player fouled out and was replaced by a player from the bench. With seven seconds remaining in the game, the opposing team tied the game. It was crunch time! The substitute player caught the inbound pass and drove full-speed down court, scoring the game-winning basket. The entire crowd erupted into pandemonium. This bench warmer had become an instant hero, but for the *opposing* team. Due to a momentary lapse in focus he had gone the wrong way, scoring the winning basket for the other team. Like playing sports well, learning well requires focused attention.

Focus is a choice you consciously make to direct your mind toward a specific purpose. When in focus, you concentrate 100 percent on the task right in front of you and nothing else. When you read, you read with total concentration. When you listen, you listen with full concentration.

It only takes a split second to lose focus and slip off purpose, but it also takes just a split second to get back on. It is much like driving a car; when the car wanders a little to the left or right, you correct the steering and stay on course (purpose). Simple — just focus one second at a time.

Focus Self-Talk
Self-talk for focus employs language such as, "I will remain mentally alert and focused for the next 20 minutes. After that time, I will challenge my mind by quizzing myself for 10 minutes over the material I just covered. At the end of this session I will know this so well I could teach it to someone else."

Self-Quizzing Promotes Focus
Spend approximately 25 to 50 percent of your allotted study time quizzing yourself over material you have just covered. Self-quizzing keeps your mind focused and provides hard evidence of what you learned and what remains to be learned.

How Do You Know When You Are Focused?
Reports from students who learned to focus well:

> *"I'm mentally 100-percent involved in what I am studying."*
> *"I'm like a sponge — soaking up as much meaning as I can, every second."*
> *"Someone could drive a Harley through the living room and I wouldn't hear it."*

Creating A "Workout" Mindset
Activate personal resources to best ensure you achieve your optimum performance. Personal resources you can activate:

- energy
- interest
- clarity
- alertness
- tenacity
- focus
- persistence

Hone your personal resources by using them, and maximize your innate potential!

Exercise 10: Focusing Your Attention

For your next study session, totally focus your mind on your assignment. Devote 100 percent awareness to what you are studying and see how long you can remain mentally connected. If your mind begins to drift, do an awareness check. Ask yourself, "Where is my attention going right now?" Direct yourself back on task. Get in the habit of making awareness checks to avoid losing time to mental drift.

Be a Power Learner - Push the Limits of Your Mind

Your goal is to become a more powerful learner. Set up intellectual workouts and challenge your brain to think. Achieve your goal by committing to a rigorous mental workout schedule that actively *engages your attention and concentration, building meaning and relevancy while making connections to prior learning.* Get ready to do your intellectual push-ups.

Developing an appreciation of how memory works and applying it to your studies is a major step in the direction of studying smarter.

Important points to consider:

- Information you read or hear begins to evaporate from short-term memory soon after you take it in (approximately 20 seconds) unless you mentally recall the new information.

- The longer you wait to work out with this new information, the more you forget. Studies have shown that we forget at least 40 to 50 percent of new information within 24 hours, unless it is mentally processed.

- Recognize that there is a difference between *review* (information coming from outside sources, e.g., book and lecture notes) vs. *mind workouts* (coming from an inner source — your mind).

Start now to turn your memory into a powerful engine for learning!

chapter 8 time management

Every Second Counts

For success in college, it is critical to manage your time effectively. Though each of us has 24 hours in a day, 168 hours in a week, the only time we actually have to work with is *now*; and each now goes by in a flash. Your challenge is to make the best use of the present. As a college student, it is crucial to invest your intellectual energy wisely. Develop a plan to schedule daily, weekly, and semester activities. Set priorities and establish goals with a timetable to achieve them. Effective *time* management promotes effective *self* management.

Many students procrastinate by allowing their state of mind or mood to dictate whether or not they study. This often leads to a sporadic, shotgun approach. Procrastinators are unwilling to abandon their comfort level to tackle rigorous academic challenge. (Refer to advantages of staying on purpose in Chapter 3.) Time management *counteracts* procrastination by:

- identifying a specific start and end time
- directing attention toward a specific purpose
- breaking tasks into more manageable ones
- focusing attention for a specified period of time
- tackling difficult subjects on time
- providing timely study breaks
- making time for leisure activities

Schedule Each Semester

Note dates on a calendar, such as due dates for term papers and when examinations are to be taken. Post the calendar on a wall where you see it every day.

Construct a Time-Budgeting Sheet as depicted on pages 64 and 65.

Write it in pencil since you may have to make changes as you go through the semester. Schedules frequently need to be modified and refined. For instance, you may need to schedule time for writing a term paper or preparing for examinations.

Schedule preparation periods just **before** discussion classes, and schedule mind workout time immediately **after** lecture classes to rehearse your notes.

- Chart your fixed time commitments such as classes, labs, and work schedule *first*.
- Set up times for essential activities for personal care, eating, and sleeping.
- Schedule specific study periods.
- Arrange time for leisure activities.

weekly: Plan your week on Sunday evenings so you are clear about your responsibilities for the coming week. Check the calendar to see if you have any exams or assignments scheduled in the near future. These will need to be added to your time-budgeting sheet so you can hit the ground running on Monday.

daily: At the beginning of each day, take five minutes and review your time-budgeting worksheet. Follow it closely. If a change needs to be made, revise your schedule to accommodate the change and still fit in your other required tasks.

time-budgeting worksheet sample

Hours	Monday	Tuesday	Wednesday	Thursday	Friday	Saturday	Sunday
8:00							
9:00							
10:00							
11:00							
12:00							
1:00							
2:00							
3:00							
4:00							
5:00							
6:00							
7:00							
8:00							
9:00							
10:00							
11:00							

completed time-budgeting worksheet sample

Hours	Monday	Tuesday	Wednesday	Thursday	Friday	Saturday	Sunday
8:00	← Breakfast / Get Ready →						↑
9:00							
10:00	Biology	ENGLISH	BIOLOGY	ENGLISH	Biology	Study Biology	
11:00	Study Biology	Study English	Study Biology	Study English	Study Biology		
12:00	← LUNCH →					LUNCH	Free Time
1:00	HISTORY	MATH	HISTORY	MATH			
2:00					prepare for bio Lab	Study Math	
3:00	Study History	Study Math	Study History	Study Math	Biology LAB	Study Hist	
4:00						↑	↓
5:00	← Dinner →						
6:00	← FREE TIME →						Prepare for Bio
7:00	Prepare for English	prepare for Bio	prepare for English	prepare for Bio	Free Time	Free Time	Prepare for History
8:00	Study & review	Study & review	Study & review	Study & review			Study & review
9:00							
10:00							
11:00					↓	↓	

STUDENT TIP:

Break Time

Be sure to take study breaks. Have set times for 5 or 10-minute breaks.

Dead Time

Dead times are gaps of time in between purposeful activity. These gaps occur every day, a few minutes here and a few minutes there. Generally speaking, they are not scheduled or routine. It is a time when we are in neutral. Your challenge is to make constructive use of dead time such as quizzing yourself over small chunks of information, organizing your notes, timed readings, written summaries, or making mind maps. Dead times bring opportunities to study or organize your notes.

Bring Dead Time to Life

Former students cited the following examples when they brought dead time to life. It was the time they spent while:

- washing clothes at the Laundromat
- picking up kids from school
- servicing the car
- sitting in a restaurant
- waiting for class to start
- sitting in a doctor or dentist office
- standing in line anywhere
- riding the bus
- taking a walk

The following are examples of proven methods as reported by students that facilitated their learning during dead times:

- **Use 3 x 5 cards.** You have a stack of 3 x 5 cards and two rubber bands. One side of each card has a question and the flip side has the answer. The initial stack of cards is called the "I don't know stack." The object of the exercise is to decrease the number of cards in the "don't know" stack and increase the number of cards in the "do know" stack. Use one rubber band for each stack. You can easily carry the cards in a pocket and pull them out during a dead time.

- **Pick a topic and summarize it.** Select a key topic from your lecture notes or a textbook and immediately write a paragraph describing or defining the concept. Don't worry about spelling or grammar. The purpose is to produce accurate information in a short period of time.

- **Make mind maps.** Mind mapping is a fun way to rehearse and review content during dead time. It is a useful study strategy developed by Tony Buzan, a leading authority on the brain and learning techniques. He is the author of *Use Both Sides of Your Brain, Use Your Perfect Memory, Mind Mapping, and Speed Reading.*

"There is a proper dignity and proportion to be observed in the performance of every act of life."
— Marcus Aurelius

Mind mapping frees your mind to spontaneously release key ideas and supportive details stored in memory, creating a flow of information as one idea triggers another. It:

- allows your mind to release stored information
- aids in organizing, integrating, comparing and contrasting key concepts
- facilitates memory, innovation, and creativity that you never knew you possessed
- helps tap into your memory bank to recall and rehearse key ideas and supportive details from lecture notes and textbooks

Mind mapping automatically associates and links new information with previously-learned knowledge, thus making useful connections.

Exercise 11: Create a Mind Map
Write down a heading from your textbook or lecture notes, and draw a circle around it. Then, immediately jot down everything that comes to mind, making lines to major points. Give yourself lots of room for flowing ideas.

Productive use can be made of dead time. Have fun identifying all the dead-time opportunities in your day and put them into practice. All of these workouts are brief in time and put you in a position to think quickly and make connections to previous learning. They keep you sharp and strengthen recall.

mind map

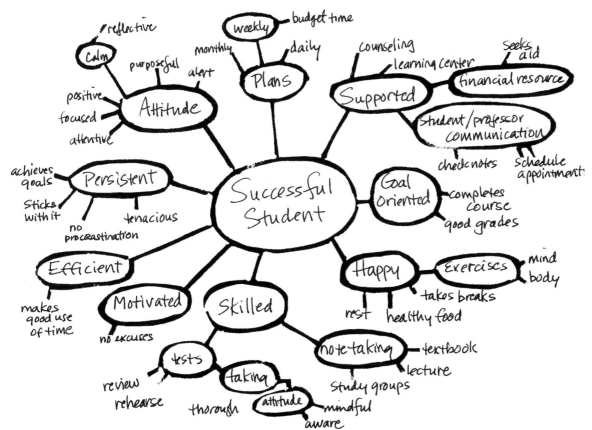

Attitude: reflective, Calm, purposeful, positive, focused, attentive, alert

Plans: weekly, budget time, monthly, daily

Supported: counseling, learning center, seeks aid, financial resource, Student/professor communication, check notes, schedule appointment

Persistent: achieves goals, Sticks with it, no procrastination, tenacious

Successful Student

Goal Oriented: completes course, good grades

Efficient: makes good use of time

Motivated: no excuses

Skilled: tests, review, rehearse, taking, thorough, Attitude, mindful, aware, note-taking, textbook, lecture, study groups

Happy: Exercises, mind, body, takes breaks, rest, healthy food

chapter 9 reading textbooks with purpose

Many students enter college from high school without a clue how to read a textbook effectively. Textbook reading requires that you read with a specific purpose and strategy. Be prepared to *work* your mind. Reading for learning, retention and recall demands clear thought, rigorous effort and powerful concentration.

Before you begin reading, ask yourself:

- What is my purpose?
- Why am I reading this?
- What do I want to accomplish?
- What will I be expected to know?
- How will I demonstrate what I know?

To get the most from your textbooks you must read actively. Good textbook reading requires mental tenacity and persistence. *Concentrate and identify key concepts, learn what they mean, and relate them to each other.* Always quiz yourself over what you have just read so it moves into long-term memory for easier recall. To make reading textbooks more interesting and meaningful you need to:

- Demonstrate a desire to improve your skills.
- Have a system that spells out how and what to do when reading a text book.
- Practice, practice, practice to become skilled at reading textbooks.

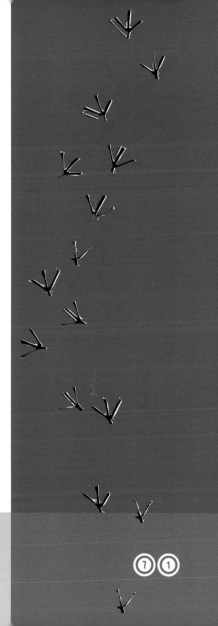

As a freshman I took a psychology course. In class I was totally absorbed with what the professor was saying. Reading the textbook, however, was another story. After about 10 minutes, my mind would begin to wander. I would daydream, become bored and frustrated, fighting to stay awake. The process was a continuous struggle. I was an aimless reader investing my time and energy, yet learning very little.

Totally lacking an effective way to read challenging textbooks, my frustration was mounting rapidly. Overwhelmed, I felt like the intellectual equivalent of a turnip. Yet I wouldn't allow myself to quit. There had to be a better way to read and learn from textbooks. I decided to ask my psychology professor for suggestions.

After class, I approached him and asked if I could discuss something of importance. I'll never forget his response. He said, *"Do you have time for a cup of coffee?"* A professor asking me, a freshman, to coffee! He was serious, and off to the cafeteria we went, got our coffee, and sat down at a table a bit away from the crowd. After a brief exchange of words, I expressed my frustration about reading textbooks. He asked me to open my psychology text and demonstrate how I read. After a few minutes he said, *"No wonder you are discouraged; you're reading it like a novel rather than a textbook. One of the best ways to bore yourself is to read a textbook like a novel. Novels are read for entertainment and relaxation while textbooks are read to gain knowledge."* In other words, activate your mind; be alert, ask questions, and search for meaningful information and answers.

STUDENT TIP:

Read the side notes in the margins of textbooks.

Many textbooks have extra notes; take advantage of these.

He informed me I wasn't alone; several students had expressed similar concerns, so he was offering a workshop. The topic would be "How to Read College Textbooks by Using the SQ3R Method". I was to show up at nine o'clock with my book, pen, notebook, and an eager mind.

SQ3R System
The SQ3R system for reading textbooks has been researched and demonstrated to be a very effective strategy for reading college textbooks. **SQ3R** stands for **Survey, Question, Read, Recite, and Review**. This system was developed by Francis Robinson (1970), a leading authority on study strategies, and the author of *Effective Study*.

By practicing the SQ3R reading strategy, my reading became more interesting and meaningful. My learning and retention increased as evidenced by improved test scores. I had learned a system for reading textbooks that not only increased my learning, but also made the study process more satisfying. I also began to learn that I was smarter than I thought. I learned what worked and I did it!

The SQ3R method facilitates understanding and meaning. It aids the movement of new information from short-term to long-term memory for more permanent storage and easier recall. The following steps are designed to help you capture and make sense of college level textbook reading in a systematic way:

"Education is the passport to the future, for tomorrow belongs to those who prepare for it today."
— Malcolm X

Step 1: **Survey**

Quickly survey the chapter to get an overview and awareness of key concepts. Read the introductory paragraph(s) at the beginning of the chapter. Quickly scan the chapter for headings, charts, graphs, bold or italicized print. This key information is important to know. Read the chapter summary and questions at the end of the chapter. Keep your eyes and mind moving forward, even if you have to push yourself to finish. Pushing your mind keeps you alert.

Step 2: **Question**

Return to the beginning of the chapter. Find the heading to the first section and turn it into a question. Start your questions with what, how, why, where, when, or who. The heading should indicate what kind of question to ask. Questions force you to think and challenge the power and limits of your mind. The process of questioning and answering establishes a deeper understanding and builds knowledge. Questions pique your curiosity, sharpen your focus, and direct your attention. Therefore, questions keep you mentally focused and on task. Rise to the challenge!

Step 3: **Read**

Read the section to find the answer to your question(s). As you read, mark and make notations of key points you want to remember. This aids focus and concentration. It also emphasizes key information to review in preparation for examinations. For more information, see Chapter 15 on test preparation.

STUDENT TIP:

Get a head start by staying a day ahead in your reading assignments.

This will prepare you for each day's lecture.

Step 4: **Recite**
Immediately after reading a section, recite the answers to your questions without looking at your book. Better yet, write them out in your own words. This step is very critical for rapid learning and retention.

Step 5: **Review**
Quickly compare your answer(s) against your textbook. Continue on to the next section of the chapter, repeating steps 2, 3, 4 and 5. Follow this procedure to the end of the chapter. It is important to keep focused and concentrate on achieving your specific purpose. If your mind becomes fatigued, take a short three-minute break. It's just like doing push-ups: when your arms become tired, you take a break.

Bring closure to each study session by taking five to 10 minutes to write a summary of what you learned from the entire session. For example, start with the sentence fragment "This is what I learned from reading…" Again, a good rule is to keep your hand moving for five to 10 minutes without stopping to check spelling or grammar. Just keep writing down what you learned.

Other Reading Strategies
Here is another approach for reading textbooks. Begin your textbook reading with an overview of your assignment by quickly scanning the introductory paragraphs, the key ideas, charts, graphs, and chapter summaries. Now, go back to the beginning and read through the entire chapter. When reading, continuously ask questions. Questions keep you alert and focused as you search for and formulate answers to them.

"Practice, by taking thought, might little by little hammer out diverse arts."
— Virgil

Often when you come upon something of key importance, the temptation is to highlight all of the information. Instead, concentrate on highlighting key words or key points. There is a downside to highlighting: it slows you down and breaks up the flow of your reading.

A faster, more efficient method is to draw a vertical line in the margin at the edge of the page by each key point. This makes later review and rehearsal quick and efficient by making key ideas easy to identify and focus upon. Use your margins. In addition to drawing vertical lines, use your margin space to write brief notes. Writing brief notes facilitates learning and retention.

Read Textbooks With a Purpose
Be prepared to work your mind. Concentrate and:

- Know what you want to accomplish.
- Identify key concepts.
- Interpret what they mean.
- Relate them to each other.
- Know how you will demonstrate what you have learned.
  (recite, summarize, mind map, self-quiz).

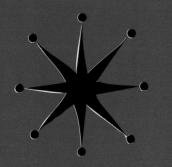

chapter 10   note-taking for lectures

Many students struggle in college because:

- They lack skills essential for taking good lecture notes.
- They do not use notes in ways that promote optimal use of memory.

Taking good lecture notes is critical for success in college — a fact I learned the hard way. In preparation for my first college exam, I read and actually studied the textbook. After the exam, I felt pretty confident in my performance. However, when the professor returned our tests, I was stunned to see a big red capital "D". My best wasn't enough and I didn't know which way to turn. Out of desperation, I spoke to the professor and asked what I could do to improve my studying. She said, "Don't worry about it; you'll just have to try harder next time."

After leaving the professor, my feelings turned from numb to rage. Try what harder and how? What did she mean, don't worry? How was I going to support my family while experimenting at trying harder?

I shared my dilemma with my neighbor who had previously taken the course from the same professor. He looked at my notes and said, "You have about a D's worth here. This professor tests primarily from her lecture notes. So when she walks into the room and says, 'Good morning,' you better write it down because it's likely to be on the test." I followed his advice and earned a B on the next test. I was no smarter, I had just learned to take better notes. I learned two things from this episode: first, find out what the professor expects and second, take good notes.

Prior to the lecture, energize and tune your thinking so you are ready to capture the key ideas. The most important part about note taking during a lecture is identifying what to write down! It's not always obvious. For a lecture, there are several clues to identifying the professor's key points and supportive details. For example, a key point is being presented when the professor says, "Pay attention to this," or "This is really important." When the professor raises his or her voice, repeats it, speaks more swiftly, or makes hand gestures, this indicates strong feeling and thus is important information.

Details supporting key concepts are often expressed with less emphasis, but they explain the key concept. Don't get smothered by the details at the expense of missing the key concepts. For example, if your psychology professor is talking about memory and forgetting, he or she will probably emphasize short-term memory, working memory, and long-term memory. Those are the key points. He or she will follow those key points with specific details of each, and your notes will have brief explanations next to each, such as capacity, duration, attention, and association.

The Cornell System of note-taking is very effective for recording lecture notes in a clear, concise, and organized format. Walter Pauk (1974) developed this system for students at Cornell University, and this approach provides a means for quick, easy review and recall of the material you have recorded. Consequently, meaningful learning is accomplished in less time.

Go to Class!

Attend all of your classes and show up early.

The Cornell System

Using a spiral notebook or a three-ringed binder with lined 8½ by 11-inch sheets of paper:

- Open to the first blank page.

- Measure 2½ inches from the left side of the page and draw a vertical line from the top to the bottom of the page. This will give you a 2½-inch column on the left side of your paper (the quiz column) and a 6-inch column on the right side (the key ideas column). See examples on pages 80 and 81.

- Throughout class, record your notes in the right column and leave the left column (the quiz column) blank until after class.

- Leave a blank space between key concepts, topics, and points that the professor makes. This is not always easy to do at first, but becomes easier with practice. Leaving a blank space will help you identify the key concepts later.

- As soon as possible after class, review your notes, looking for those key points. Turn each key point into a question and record it in the left column. For example, if you are studying psychology and the topic covered is classical conditioning, you might write in the left column, "How would you describe classical conditioning? What are the key points?" When turning key points into questions, begin your questions with what, why, how, where, when, or who.

This process gets you thinking about the content of your notes right away without having to rely on memorizing everything. Just by organizing your notes, you begin to make sense of them.

Going over your notes and *writing* questions about each key idea and *answering* your questions *right away* strengthens your understanding, retention, and recall.

Students reported that once they became competent in this system, it only took them five to ten minutes after class to identify key points. Soon, you should realize positive outcomes.

If your notes are difficult to read, rewrite them daily in the Cornell System. Just the act of rewriting your notes enables you to learn more, retain more information, and make recall and review easier.

By using the Cornell System of note-taking, you establish a format of questions where the answers are provided on the same page. This provides you the opportunity to quickly quiz yourself and immediately check your answers. Develop the habit of doing this each day as soon after class as possible to prevent from forgetting the information.

Making the Information Stick
For learning and optimal retention, it is critical to recall and review small chunks of information frequently. Rehearse your lecture note questions and answers on a regular basis so the information becomes a part of your long-term memory. Rather then cramming and overloading your memory, distributing your self-quizzes over a scheduled period of time strengthens retention and recall, which helps make the information stick.

The following pages show two examples of how to apply the Cornell System:

lecture notes from study skills class

Quiz Column	Key Ideas
How do you read a textbook?	To read a textbook, you must be prepared to work at what you are reading
What key points do I need to keep in mind while I am reading?	*While you read:* • consider your purpose • what you need to accomplish • what you need to know
What is SQ3R?	*SQ3R Stands for:* • Survey: overview of chapter • Questions: creating questions (before reading) about the chapter topics • Read: to answer your questions • Recite: Recite your answers (without looking at the book), then write them in your own words. • Review: compare your answer with the textbook, then repeat the SQ3R process with each chapter section. At the end of the chapter (or study session) write a quick summary of what you have learned.
What is the benefit of SQ3R?	You can use SQ3R to study for tests. SQ3R helps you learn versus memorize. Rehearsing short chunks of information immediately after reading moves information into long term memory.
How does SQ3R become a learning habit?	Practice SQ3R to make the learning process a habit and routine.

lecture notes from anatomy and physiology class

Quiz Column	Key Ideas
What is heart disease?	Heart disease is the blockage of coronary arteries which supply blood to the heart.
Name four things that reduce heart disease:	*Reduce Heart Disease by:* • eating a low fat, low sodium diet • exercising regularly • reducing stress • keeping your weight at a normal level • not smoking
How do heart attack symptoms vary from men to women?	*Just before and during a heart attack, women commonly experience:* • shortness of breath • weakness • unusual fatigue *Just before or during a heart attack, men commonly experience:* • pain and discomfort in the center of the chest • discomfort in the arms, back, neck, jaw, or stomach • shortness of breath • a cold sweat • nausea or light-headedness
True or false? The heart is a muscle with 4 chambers.	True. The heart has 4 chambers; two atria (left and right) and two ventricle (left and right).
Essay: Describe how the blood flows through the cardiovascular system.	De-oxygenated blood flows in Venae Cavae veins to right atrium. Right atrium squeezes de-oxygenated blood to the right ventricle. Right ventricle sends blood through pulmonary artery to lungs. Pulmonary vein carries oxygenated blood from lungs to left atrium. Left atrium contracts and sends oxygenated blood to left ventricle. Left ventricle pumps blood into the aorta which branches off and carries oxygenated blood to the rest of the body.

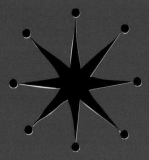

Plan, Don't Cram

Study something every day. Don't wait until the last minute to "cram" for a test.

Focus on key subject areas and main topics. Read end-of-chapter summaries and do end of-chapter questions. Quiz yourself with your Cornell method study notes.

Learn your study techniques and stick with them.

Exercise 12: Make a Self-Quiz

- *Right after class: Turn key points into questions and quiz yourself.*
- *Three days later: Review and quiz yourself.*
- *One week later: Review and quiz yourself.*

chapter II study, review, and workout cycle

The study, review and workout cycle helps prepare your mind immediately prior to class, suggests what to do while in class and immediately following class, and helps you prepare for examinations on a weekly schedule.

Each step prepares you for the next phase leading right up to examination time.

1. DAILY
Immediately prior to class — quick review:
Arrive to class a few minutes early. Sharpen your focus by taking out your notes from the previous day's class and reviewing them prior to the beginning of class. If you have any questions, ask the professor for clarification.

In class — be alert:
Take charge of your physical and mental state of alertness. For example:

- physically assume an alert posture
- mentally keep a sharp, clear mind by directing your total attention to what the instructor is saying
- resolve to maintain focused attention; act as if the instructor is talking directly to you

"Assume a virtue, if you have it not."
— William Shakespeare

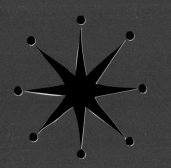

Capture the *meaning* of what is being taught and record key information. If you have to make a choice between recording key points or details, go for the key points. Then, ask for the information that is not clear. Or, after class, make it your job to ask the professor for details, or look for them in your reading.

Immediately following class — quick review and workout:
Review your notes for 5 to 10 minutes. Using the Cornell Note-Taking Method, identify three to 10 key points and record them in question form in the left hand quiz column. Right after that, do a mind workout by quizzing yourself over these concepts for a minimum of five minutes. Answer the questions, from memory, *without* referring to your notes. This provides feedback showing precisely what you do and do not know. Mark a plus sign for the questions you answered correctly, and a minus sign for those you missed and focus on these.

2. END OF WEEK
At the end of each week, test your knowledge by constructing a self-quiz. Pull questions from the quiz column of your daily notes for that week. Take your quiz, writing the answers without the aid of your notes. Check your answers against your notes and textbook. To determine if your questions are challenging enough, show them to your instructor to get feedback. Save these weekly quizzes for pre-exam review and rehearsal. You will have quizzed yourself several times before the instructor tests you.

3. PRE-EXAM

Several days before the formal exam, review text, notes and self-quizzes. Build a comprehensive test from your weekly self-quizzes, emphasizing the questions you had difficulty answering. Take your test and identify where your knowledge is still weak. Work on the areas that you need to strengthen.

4. EXAM

During the exam, be alert and focused. Remind yourself that you have prepared well, and this is your opportunity to demonstrate what you know.

STUDENT TIP:

When taking tests, make sure you thoroughly read the directions and answer all the questions.

Check the back of the exam, too!

chapter 12 strategies and tips for math success

Often students decide that certain subjects are difficult, which practically ensures avoidance and failure. Math is often one of those subjects — yet we use math in one form or another every single day. Math can be learned — no special talent or gift required! Below, you'll find numerous suggestions to become that math whiz you thought was someone else. Kaye Tavernier, a math instructor at Cook County High School in Grand Marais, Minnesota, lends these suggestions:

Practice Good Math Habits

1. Use a pencil, **not a pen.** You will make mistakes; the teacher does too.

2. Be neat and organized in work. Write numbers and symbols clearly so there is no confusion later. Be especially careful of: 4 and 9, 1 and 7, 5 and S, x and y.

3. Draw a picture. Sketch to help "see" the info given and the solution to be found.

4. Always show your work. Except in the case of simple mental math, show your work. (Skipping steps often leads to errors.)

5. Calculate carefully. When using a calculator, be careful to correctly enter the problem. Don't throw away the calculator instruction book!

6. Use the appropriate unit. Always label answers with the appropriate unit.

"Education is the ability to listen to almost anything without losing your temper or your self-confidence."
— Robert Frost

7. **Learn vocabulary.** Record and review new math vocabulary regularly. Make flashcards if needed.

8. **Keep up with daily work.** More than any other subject, math is learned by doing. Math learning is cumulative. What you learn tomorrow is an extension of what you learned today.

9. **Ask questions.** Don't be afraid to ask questions. Be specific in what you do not understand or did not follow in the lesson.

10. **Estimate.** Estimate to check reasonableness of answers. Does your answer make sense?

11. **Study for math tests.** Review past homework, notes, and vocabulary. Work through review problems at the end of the chapter or unit.

Practice these skills until proficient:

1. Mental math — basic math facts, multiply/divide with powers of 10
2. Divisibility rules for 2, 3, 5, 10, and others
3. Have sense of size of common measuring units, metric and standard
4. Know common measurement equivalents
5. Add, subtract, multiply, and divide with whole numbers

6. Add, subtract, multiply, and divide with decimal numbers
7. Add, subtract, multiply, and divide with common fractions
8. Understand place value through millions and millionths
9. Be able to read very large and very small numbers
10. Use formulas for solving common application problems
11. Solving the three main types of percent problems: (find the percent, find the 100-percent number, find the partial-percent number.)

Maintain a "can do" attitude

- Everyone can do math!
- Recognize and accept that math is part of our daily lives in work and play.
- Math is a process — there is more than one way to arrive at a solution.
- Develop a confidence in problem-solving strategies. This is more important than just getting the "right" answer.
- Take advantage of tutoring help available and math-help websites.

chapter 13 student and instructor communication

To get clear about whether your approach to studying adequately meets the expectations of your instructor, select a challenging class and schedule an appointment with your instructor to discuss your study methods. By doing this, you gain your instructor's undivided attention for a specific block of time. This investment of 15 to 20 minutes of your time often pays off in terms of how to direct your mental effort. You send a clear message to your instructor of your strong commitment to the course, and your instructor also gets to know you as a person.

Bring your lecture notes to the appointment. Inform your instructor that you want to learn as much as possible in the course. Do *not* say you want to get an A or B in the class, since this is the last thing your instructor will want to hear. If you clearly understand the instructor's expectations, you will better know what to concentrate on and study more efficiently.

To help determine if you meet your instructor's expectations for a high level of performance, present your notes to your instructor and ask the following questions:

1. "Are these notes comprehensive and thorough enough?" (Wait for instructor to respond.)

2. Follow up with, "Do you have any suggestions on how I could take better notes?"

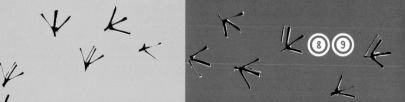

3. Next, take out your self-quizzes and present them to your instructor. Ask, "Are these questions rigorous enough to adequately challenge my thinking in preparation for a test?" (Watch for a surprised response from the instructor, since this may be the first time a student has ever presented him or her with a self-quiz.)

4. Follow up with, "How could I ask better questions to master the material?"

As part of the Academic Fitness program I taught, I would assign students the task of going to see the instructor. Students dreaded it. However, once they had completed it, they reported very favorable results. They seemed to be surprised with the fact that the instructor was "human". Instructors were impressed that students took the initiative to come in, share their notes, and ask how to improve them. Instructors were particularly impressed when they saw students' self-quizzes and were helpful in providing additional tips. Take this step, and you will find that the positive results are well worth the effort.

"Knowing others is intelligence; knowing yourself is true wisdom. Mastering others is strength; mastering yourself is true power."
— Lao Tzu Laozi

chapter 14   studying in the virtual world

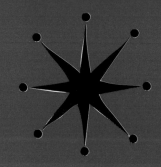

Online education may fit your life better than an on-campus classroom. Here are some reasons students offer for doing all or some of their coursework online:

- flexibility with work and family schedules
- location: the nearest college or university is a long way away
- choice: the nearest college or university may not have the program of study you want
- quality: you want to attend a prestigious school, but can only do so online
- affordability: moving to the campus and living in a dorm is not an option
- accessibility: you have limited mobility, and online education provides immediate access

One important thing to keep in mind is that taking an online class can be harder than taking the class in person. There is usually much more reading, more assignments, and more discussion. It takes more time. The myth that online classes are easier is just that: a myth. While many students would prefer to be in a real-time classroom, the flexibility of online and other virtual learning is attractive. At the same time, online or other distance education classes rely heavily on your ability to be self-motivated and self-disciplined. While the beauty of taking an online course allows you to keep your own schedule, keeping to that schedule can be extremely challenging. It is very important to plan and be organized.

Access to technology is also an important consideration. If you have high-speed Internet access you will experience fewer problems than if you have dial-up or satellite service. If you have slow

STUDENT TIP:

Help Yourself

Seek help early before you get swamped. Most colleges offer a free tutoring service.

access, find a location with high-speed access as an alternative. Taking exams or viewing video clips is difficult if you are using dial-up, since the service could be dropped or interrupted while you are in the process of taking your test, and it can take 45 minutes to download a short video clip. This leaves you wondering whether the task was done or the assignment received. It's a good idea to talk to your local library, high school, or employer to see if you can schedule computer use for more consistent Internet access.

If you have the opportunity, talk to someone who has taken an online class *before* your course begins. You will also save yourself a lot of time by becoming familiar with the course website. Each college or university works with a particular platform to deliver the course via the Web to you. There will be specific systems to learn that will enable you to participate in discussions, submit assignments and take exams. Your college will have an online "tutoring" session or program that will give you the opportunity to explore the course home page. Take the time to check this out! Online courses have specific locations for posting discussion topics, weekly assignments, submitting homework, and taking quizzes. Make sure you know where these items are located before starting the course. You don't want to put yourself in the position of learning the technology and the course content all at once. This will save you a lot of time in the long run.

Short checklist for a virtual course:

- Become familiar with the technology before you start the course. For instance, if you are taking a course via interactive television or webcam, make sure you understand how the equipment works.

- Keep your syllabus handy so you can keep track of deadlines (just like with an on-campus course). You will not receive credit for late work.

- Login to your online class the first day of class as early as possible. This will give you a chance to make sure you have the correct ID and passwords to access your class. The first assignment will be posted, which is sometimes just participating in a discussion to introduce yourself and get to know your classmates.

- Check your e-mail as often as possible for changes to the syllabus or other additional information from your instructor.

Your online class will have a course syllabus, just like an on-campus course. While an online course is flexible, this does not mean you can do the assignments whenever you want. Your flexibility is more about when you check in during the day or week. Follow the syllabus closely and plan your assignments and tests around specific deadlines. If you can, check in daily on your

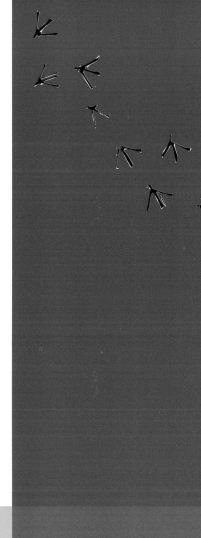

course home page to detect changes in the assignments, due dates, or announcements. Make sure you know where your professor is posting information! Sometimes, teachers will use multiple locations on the course website to post information, including your school e-mail account, so check this regularly.

Class participation happens by using chat rooms, course blogs, or discussion boards, and this can be a significant portion of your grade. Just as if you are sitting in a classroom, teachers will check and see how much you are participating in class. Feel free to e-mail your instructor with questions or ideas, and make sure you make contact with your instructor on a regular basis.

Tests occur in online courses, just as for in-class courses. These tests are administered online, although some of your exams will be "proctored" and some will not. A proctor is someone (not a relative or friend) who is given the password to your test and oversees you taking the test. Proctors can usually be found at nearby schools, libraries, or higher-education institutions. Often this involves some paperwork, so plan plenty of time to take care of these details.

Typically, exams (usually quizzes) that are not proctored will be shorter. There is usually a time limit, which means you will have to be very familiar with the material. Even though you can use notes or your book, you will rarely have enough time to search those materials for answers. Since the exam is administered online, see if you can determine ahead of time whether you can go back and change answers as you are going through the exam. Some tests allow you to do this; others do not. With online classes, it is critical to turn in your assignments and take your exams on time.

Pay close attention to those deadlines and plan appropriately. If for some reason you cannot take an exam before a scheduled deadline, contact your instructor as soon as you can. There may be an opportunity to keep the exam time open long enough for you to take it at another time.

You will need to practice the same study habits for your distance education classes as you would for in-class courses. And just like a traditional course, your mental attitude and your study strategies will make all the difference in your success.

chapter 15   test preparation

Test preparation should start on day one of each course. Establish a clear understanding of when exams are scheduled; mark the dates on your calendar and time-budgeting worksheets. By being prepared, you reduce test-taking anxiety.

You should be in good shape to prepare for course examinations if your instructor(s) approved your lecture notes as comprehensive, and self-quiz questions as challenging. (Refer to Chapter 13 regarding Student and Instructor Communication.) Daily rehearsal of lecture and textbook notes, plus the rehearsal of weekly self-quizzes should leave you well prepared to start serious preparation for examinations. Review textbook chapters emphasizing major headings, key ideas, and chapter summaries, especially the study and rehearse techniques in Chapter 11. If study guides have been provided, review and rehearse them.

Instructors often have a unique style of testing. You can learn from other students who have had the same instructor in the past. Having access to previous tests can also provide information on how a specific instructor tests. Once you take a test from your instructor you will know his or her style.

Tips for Taking Examinations
View test taking as an opportunity to express what you know. The key to taking tests successfully is to be well prepared. Thorough preparation is also an effective way to reduce test anxiety. Most students experience some tenseness before an exam. A moderate amount of anxiety is good because it helps to keep you alert for the test. However, excessive anxiety may hamper your performance.

"It is a rough road that leads to the heights of greatness."
— Seneca

To help reduce anxiety, do the following:

1. Calm and relax yourself by taking a few slow, deep breaths, exhaling gently while at the same time allowing your shoulders to sag in a relaxed manner. Notice any tension in your body and relax those muscles.

2. Upon receiving your exam, quickly scan it to determine the amount of time needed to answer each question. Answer the questions you know first, then go back and answer the questions that you have to think about. Stay calm and alert. Sometimes there are clues on following questions that will help you answer previous questions that you left blank. *Note: Some online tests do not allow you to go back to answer earlier questions, and you will have to answer each question as you go through the test.*

3. Read the directions thoroughly! There may be multiple parts to the question. For instance, your instructor may ask a question, and then ask you to elaborate on your response and provide specific examples.

4. If the directions say, "Show all of your work," make sure you put your work on the *answer sheet*, not on the test booklet.

5. Use the allotted time that is allowed for the exam. You do not need to be one of the first few out of the room. From my experience in administering exams, students who used the allotted time period frequently scored well.

Here are some examples of different types of tests and test questions:

Two Types of Tests:

Objective tests often test for details and specifics:
- multiple choice
- true/false
- matching questions

Subjective tests require knowledge of general concepts:
- written essays
- short answer

Tips for Answering Multiple Choice Questions
This is where you need to use your critical thinking skills.

- Answer questions in sequence, but skip those you are unsure of and come back to them later. Avoid spending excessive time on any one question.
- Try answering the question before looking at the multiple choice answers.
- Be sure to read all of the choices before you select your answer, since two choices may be correct, but one would be more correct than the other.

- If you are unsure of an answer, first rule out the ones you know are wrong and then select the answer you believe to be most correct.
- Be sure you fully understand the questions before you answer them.

Sample Multiple Choice Question:

As opposed to essay exams, which generally require you to write your answers in sentence form, multiple choice questions require you to:

A. Provide answers from which you identify and select the correct answer.
B. Choose the <u>most</u> correct answer between two correct answers.
C. Provide a short explanation.
D. Both A and B

The correct answer is D.

Tips for Answering True/False Questions

- If one part is false, the entire question is false.
- Watch for words that indicate *absolutes* such as every, all, never, none, or always, which frequently indicates that the statement is false.
- Words like usually, seldom, perhaps, some, or maybe (not absolutes) are often true statements.

Sample True/False Questions:

True/false

_____1. All college students graduate in four years.

_____2. Some college students graduate in four years.

The correct answer for #1 is False. The correct answer for #2 is True.

Tips for Answering Matching Questions:

- Read both columns first.
- Connect the answer to the correct statement.
- Do the ones you know first. This process will narrow down the choices that may lead to clues for the remaining matches.

Sample Matching Question:

Match the following items:

_____1. SQ3R   a. excellent system for note-taking

_____2. Cornell System   b. method of review and recall

_____3. 3 x 5 cards   c. effective way to gain feedback

_____4. Student-Instructor conference   d. effective reading strategy for textbooks

The correct answers are: 1. d, 2. a, 3. b, 4. c.

Tips for Answering Essay Questions

- Read the directions very carefully so you know what is required. Watch for key words such as justify, define, explain, compare, contrast, describe, or summarize.
- Quickly read the questions and determine the points allotted and the amount of time you can devote to each one.
- Do not rewrite the question; it simply eats up the clock.
- Make a brief outline of key ideas for each question to set up an appropriate sequence to follow before you start writing the answer. Some students write the key ideas in the margins of their test papers. This demonstrates to the instructor that you knew where you were going — that you had the key concepts.
- Write out your answer in full. Avoid unnecessary fluff; be clear, specific, and concise.
- When you have finished writing your essay, proofread your answers, making any changes or modifications that would strengthen your answer.

Sample Essay Question:
What specifically can you do to reduce forgetfulness and increase retention of information?

Answer: Use the tips above to answer this one yourself!

Tips for Answering Short-Answer Questions

- Use your 3 x 5 cards to be well prepared for your test.
- Use mind maps to thoroughly understand your material.
- Use your Cornell System notes to quiz yourself before the test so that the information is fresh in your mind.
- Read the test questions very carefully to make sure you understand what they are asking.
- Underline or highlight key words or terms in the test question.

Sample Short-Answer Test Questions:

1. How soon is it likely that a student will begin to forget content following a lecture or after reading textbook material, even if they had taken good notes?_____

2. What percent of information studied, but not rehearsed, are we likely to forget within 24 hours?_____

The correct answers are:
1. Within 20 seconds,   2. 40 to 50%.

chapter 16   conclusion

The purpose of this book is to send a strong message to you, the student, that:

1. You have far more ability than you use.
2. You can learn how to study skillfully, efficiently and effectively.
3. Having learned **how** to study with skill, you will better learn **what** you are studying.
4. Your attitude plays a major role in your academic performance. Attitude provides a powerful force, influencing what you think and do as a student.

Can you be successful at college? Stop and think about it. How can you help but improve your performance when you think critically, use proven methods for reading textbooks and taking notes, quiz yourself daily, budget your time, learn test taking techniques and combine these into a well-planned and organized process?

If you have made effective use of this book and internalized its message, you should now be able to:

- read your textbooks in ways to get the most meaning from them
- take good notes, and know *how* and *when* to study them for maximum benefit
- find the power range of your memory
- think more critically
- reduce mental drift
- maintain focus

"No one can make you feel inferior without your consent."
— Eleanor Roosevelt

- quiz yourself to prepare for tests
- make good use of your dead time
- check in with your professors
- go to class!

addendum

When I was a Professor at Minnesota State University, Moorhead, students would occasionally return just to check in and let me know how they were doing, sometimes as much as a year later. They would say something surprising to me: "Bob, I don't study for grades anymore." And I would say, "That's interesting, what do you study for?" And they would respond, "I go to class, whether I am interested in that class or not, and tell myself each day I am going to get everything I possibly can from this class, and know it so well I could teach it to someone tomorrow. And guess what! The grades took care of themselves."

Students began to take responsibility for their own learning. In addition to going to class every day, they utilized a systematic approach to reading and note-taking. They also focused on staying in the moment while studying, creating questions and self-quizzes. Those students that did that, and checked in with their professors now and then, typically did well!

What was in it for me? Watching people realize they had the potential to become successful. The true beauty of a human being came out when they learned how to use their potential. I encourage you to continue honing your skills to build further competence and confidence. I extend my very best wishes to you in your journey through college and beyond.

— Bob

bibliography

Buzan, Tony, and Buzan, Barry. (1993). *The Mind Map Book*. London: BBC Books.

Ebbinghaus, Hermann. (2010). *Memory; A Contribution to Experimental Psychology*. Charleston, S.C: Nabu Press. (Original work published 1885).

Pauk, Walter. (1974). *How to Study*. Boston: Houghton Mifflin.

Robinson, Francis. (1970). *Effective Study*. 4th ed. New York: Harper and Row.

Bloom, Benjamin S. (1956).*Taxonomy of Educational Objectives*. Boston: Allyn and Bacon.

index